Mum and Dad went shopping.

2

They took Adam and Yasmin.

Mum wanted a kettle.

Adam wanted to go home.

Yasmin wanted some shoes.

Adam was bored.

Dad wanted a track suit.

Adam was fed up.

Adam was tired.

He went into a tent.

Mum and Dad looked for Adam.

They couldn't find him.

14

Everyone looked for Adam.

Adam was fast asleep.